AF439846

A Letter to You

DARIUS STRONG

LOLA WRITES

A LETTER TO YOU

Darius Strong & Lola Writes

ISBN: 9798434106788

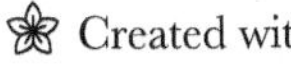 Created with Vellum

CONTENTS

Acknowledgments

Thank you for pouring love into me so that I can love myself
- Darius

I'll love, love forever, no matter how much love hates me
- Lola

CRUSH PHASE

———

<u>Petrichor</u>
/ˈpeˌtrîkôr/
noun
a pleasant smell that frequently accompanies the
first rain after a long period of warm, dry
weather.

be
mine

SOULMATE

My soulmate
My God given partner in life
God handpicked you personally for me
To have and to hold in holy matrimony
We're so young and have so much life to live
But it feels like we're supposed to live it together
All the trials and tribulations that we go through,
we're supposed to go through it together
All the successes that God blesses us with,
We're supposed to witness them together
All the big news in our life are supposed to
be shared with each other
You belong to meAnd I belong to you
It just seems like that's how it's supposed to be
All the hurt and the pain will be worth it
All the time and effort will be rewarded
Love will be enough for us to last
Because we're supposed to last

DATING PHASE

Zugzwang
zəg͵zwaNG, ˈtso͞og͵tsvaNG/
noun
a situation in which the obligation to make a
move in one's turn is a serious, often decisive,
disadvantage.

QUAKE

Please grace me with your fondest memory
Don't let it get distorted as you sing.
A thought the covers you up, a tender thing,
And kisses you with warmth - how you should me. Share with me
what horrors plague your poor head.
Make me weep with what sorrows distress you
Smother me with the pains that bring you blues
So that your walls will bother me instead.
The things I know about you show much progress
But I fear you won't keep pushing forward
The worry is weighing down on you are strong
I swear I'll bring happiness to us both
What gives me vigor are your sad, sad words
Trust me - your problems won't stay very long

FULL DISCLOSURE

Only after our hasty interview
I'll have enough to think of you.
I've thought in wholly and thought it through.
Discover my car in your window's view
Run outside into the street
By my side's your rightful seat
Sit back, stay calm, don't even speak.
Seal the doors, crash into me.
They tore your heart an agony
But you love me so, this casually.
You shut your eyes, saw love with me
Blinded it from such casualties.
I'll conceal myself deep in your bones.
Motion to repeat as were oceanic zones.
Frantic pleas thrown off by sirens tone,
Take a plunge into what's unknown
Forget your plans, leave all postponed.
Covered in my skin's cologne,
I watch you begin to moan.

CAN YOU?

Can you stimulate my soul?
Make love to my mind?
Can you take my brain places where it's never been?
Stroke deep into my thoughts
Create memories that last a lifetime
Give me that tingling sensation from my head to my body just by
the words that comes out of your mouth
I want your voice to send Shockwaves to my brain and give me
goosebumps
Take me on a spiritual high
Enlighten my soul with your wisdom
Show me your knowledge and I'll show you mine
Give me what I've been yearning for all my life

SHAPE ME

Even concrete has a time of unsettling uncertainty

But after it settles it knows what it is

When can my thoughts settle?

When will my ways congeal?

I can't be sculpted after I become concrete

But what if-

I don't want to be stiff

Concrete settle so gracefully

Yet you shape me so banefully

RUSSIAN ROULETTE

Love is full of risks

Possibilities of getting hurt

The maybes and maybe nots are overwhelming

Love is full of what ifs

What if they're not the one

What if it's fate for us to be

What if love just isn't enough

It's hard to play it safe when it comes to love

There's no set plan in order to not get hurt

There's no blueprint so you don't hurt your soulmate

You just gotta take that chance

Close your eyes and take a deep breath

And when you jump, pray someone will catch you

Sometimes you get hurt

Sometimes you're the one who hurts them

Do you give up

Or do you try just one more time

True love is everlasting

It's unconditional

It's accepting,

It's beautiful

I guess that's what makes the journey worth it

All the heartache,

All the beatings

All the pain

HONEYMOON PHASE

Sisu
— see'-soo

noun

strength of will, determination, perseverance, and acting rationally in the face of adversity. It is not momentary courage, but the ability to sustain that courage.

HE SAY

He says he wanna taste my cookies
He say I gotta be sweet
With all that caramel dripping down to my feet
Well what about me? …
What about that twinkle in my eyes?
Have you even noticed my sparkling smile?
You say you love every bit of me… but why?
Is it my charisma that lures you in?
Or is it simply how it jiggles when I walk away?
What exactly are you trying to win?
My heart or an easy way to get in
The gold that lies between my thighs
The pearls that sit high beyond man's touch
Yea I know my sweet taste can give you a high
Why can't my love be enough?

WILLIE WONKS

Haiku lines are Wands

Some seven along, some five

It's motion that counts

ALL
BECAUSE
THEY
MET
AND
FELL
in love

CRIME MOB

I straddled the thought

Of you and steer it until

I cum of chaste sense

PROTEASES

My bed is a place

Where my thoughts run off into

My vivid nightmares

FOREPLAY

Slowly caress my thoughts
Tickle my sweet spot in my mind
Arouse my brain by your words

Explore my mind
Dive into my brain
Fill me up with your wisdom

Stroke deep into my thoughts
Penetrate my mind with your knowledge
Kiss me with your charm

Our minds intertwined
Our words twisting and turning together
Forming such beautiful, intellectual, conversations

Make love to my mind
Dive deep into my soul
Simulate my mind

CRAVINGS

I've pictured the day I get to see you over and over in my head
Different scenarios, but they all end in the same fashion
You pick me up in your car from the airport
You open the door as I'm standing on the other side of your home
I'm shaking from the butterflies leading a revolt against my stomach
Your bright eyes and warm smile create a peaceful harmony
amongst the butterflies
I feel awkward, not knowing whether I should hug your or reach my
hand out for
you to shake or pucker my lips

You pull me in and sweep me off my feet in a big embrace
Your hand wrapped around my waist and my legs wrapped around
yours
My mind is throbbing with the lustful thoughts consuming, taking
every inch of me
The next few hours are of us conversing and drinking, relaxing our
bodies and minds
I already know I'll feel so comfortable in your presence, like we've
known each other all our lives

Then the cravings start...
I'm staring deep into your chocolate brown eyes
I'm watching your perfectly shaped lips, but I no longer hear the
words coming out of your mouth
All I hear are the thoughts of my inner vixen telling me to get closer,
touch here, caress him there
These thoughts are taking over my soul, trying to get me to seduce
you the way you've always done with your words alone
I've always been very open about expressing my sexual needs to you

I was never silent about how I want you to caress my pearls while
you twirl...
But at this moment I'm frozen...
I'm not sure how to tell you how I want our tongues intertwined as
we passionately kiss
My lips can't form the words to say I want you looking deep into my
eyes while you're deep inside me
I'm terrified to call you anything besides your name, out of fear that
daddy will slip through my lips instead
I don't even want to come too close for fear that our hands might
accidentally touch, and an electrified chill runs through my spine

Lord knows I crave your touch
I crave your kisses
I crave your intimacy
I crave your time and attention
I wish somehow, someway soon you could be mine, all mine
I don't want to share you with anyone else
I want you to love me again, like you did before
Tell me how I'm your soulmate just one more time

OBOE

Glide down your coal licorice,

like tears rushing away.

From the blues.

WANDERLUST

I want to get lost in your haze.
I want you and your body for days,
I daze and doze, I rose from my stupor.
Suppressed voices and muffled moans from beneath the sheets
Make me feel almost complete.
There's no need to compete for my affection, you've earned it.
You and your connection, leads me in a different direction and-
I'm left to wonder who's next to be-

Mine.

SHE DOESN'T LOVE ME BACK.
AND SHE NEVER WILL.

DISILLUSIONMENT PHASE

---

la locura tocando mi Puerta—

Madness knocking on my door

JUNE 25TH

Depression takes the soul of others, but no effect on you.
You've barred yourself in isolation in a cold dark room
And all the while you felt divine,
somethings got ahold of you.
Devil's fire in your veins.
Destruction starting to take reign.
And now you wake up. Wake up.
Two hours way past noon
You've complained this life offers you nothing,
When all you had to do was flee the room.
Leave your room.
Free of gloom.
Need a bit of fresh air; do your fair share
But you pondered the day away,
thinking of the day you'll say,
Maybe this will be the day…
But for you that day was yesterday.

LETTER FROM BAMBI

I wish you would have warned me earlier
Before I already fell in love
"Don't get to near for there's lions, beware"
Alas my love, I'm afraid I'm already in the lion's den
Tucked under your breast
Covered by your warmth
Oblivious to the fact that you were shielding me from your own
betrayal
I should have known…
Now you sing your regrets in this lullaby
Fuck your lullaby
Fuck your grandfather and his 7 wives
Fuck your jungle of women
You beautiful predator…

ABERDEEN

Eenie Meenie Mo

Should I throw a rope, catch my

Lover by their ***throat***.

JEALOUS MINDS

It haunts me in my sleep at night
I'm always wondering if I should try… again.
But no matter how hard I try
I get no reply.
He said it's because I'm jealous-who?
Not I!
I mean do you expect me to share?
Ha! I wish I might!
Let someone else in my life
Share where my heart lays down all the time
Call me stingy if you want, but you still can't have a bite
I worked hard for everything I have
And I have no problem sharing everything else, I'll be glad
But as far as this one right here? You just can't have that.
Call me mad but I just don't do that.
You can cry all you want
Send me cards or even threats if you think you tough
But nothing will be enough for me to share what was mine from the
start

RECOIL

It's days like these that I always get the best of me.
Wishing you were here next to me.
It's been yearlong since you woke up next to me.
It's not like I wasn't trying…
You just grew tired of explaining,
There's too much to say,
and I know you'll never approve of me lying.
Can't let you get away,
but it feels too late to hang on with trying.
I never really wanted to let you go,
but things have changed since my lying.
And I know if I said I missed you,
you might get the wrong impression.
So I'll keep my distance and except that I learned my lesson.

HOW
ARE
YOU,
REALLY?
THE NUE
CO
OVERALL
MURALS

Ambivalence Phase

Swinn-twa, Mô zami—

Take care, my friend'

CONTROL REAWAKENING

There's a motion in my soul
There's a soreness in my throat
A willing in my eyes,
A wail in my words— but there's also tranquility.
There's also splendor,
What is so wrong with me?
That makes me feel,
There is strength in pain
I feel this ache grabbing me
I feel this misery move thee,
Push me off the edge to fall into clarity.

PAINFUL MEMORIES

I miss you so much it hurts
My eyes swell up with tears of sorrow
My heart slowly breaking off the last little pieces
that were left

My mind filled with the pain,
that I endured losing you
Or did I ever really have you?
Did I ever have possession of your heart?

Because Lord knows you owned mine
Each tear falling from my face is a memory of you
I cringe when I picture your face because I know I'll
never see it again
My stomach turns when I reminisce the heavenly sound
of your voice

God, I miss your voice...
I've probably been forgotten by now,
A distant memory
I've gone from your soulmate
To a girl you once knew

It's true that hearts don't break even
Yours have been put back together,
with another half.
While mine is shattered to pieces
I don't even know which piece goes were anymore

You've moved on,
I have too as well
But it's difficult when all those feelings
you said you felt for me
I actually truly felt for you

PHOTOGRAPHS

Present

Not

Yore

Imprisoned inside photographs of fond memories

You, came before I in the alphabet in my mind

As I laid you to rest on sheets of paper

Mapped your outline in delicate diction

You were the life that toted the earth

THANK YOU, LOVE

You see my hate starts
where my love ends,
And when hate is dismissed
love his back again.
See love is tough
like a hard shell.
Unfamiliar though I feel like I know it well
I had doubts it could even exist
But I feel it's presents deep
Thank you love, because you persist.
The thing is,
I can't see it in others
I have faith in my sight
Till I lost another
You open my eyes
To things I couldn't see before
Did things for you
That you can never leave me for
But when time rolls by
Emotions roll out
You weren't feeling the same way

So, I had to roll out
But I found out just how true the truth is
"You don't know how good it is until you lose it"
I gave everything in front
just to get you back
Then a cold shoulder to the face
Put me on my back
Desperate to get a Queen
Back to making that honey
I gave her roof, food, and time
even save you some money
Thank you, love.
For giving me hope to resort
but in your eyes,
I was nothing but a resource
Nothing but a free ride,
an open target, dead eye.
This is the reason that I can't be a Jedi
They might control the Force
Around and above.
But the force no one controls
Are the forces of love
How rude of I
to walk within a God's fire
Though I spoke to an angel's heart
But the devil had your mind wired

RECONCILIATION PHASE

Cicatrix
/ˈsikəˌtriks/
noun
the scar of a healed wound.

WRITE ME A LOVE NOTE

Write me a love note my dear

One that would make my heart flutter

And my cheeks turn a rosy color

Make me feel like I'm the one you'll never let get away

Talk about our forever days

"Soon to come my love", is what you would say

Write me a love song

About the still waters and the hushed winds

Tell me how you can only hear our heart beats intertwine

Somewhat like a harmony

And say something like, "Our musical love is so sweet"

Tell me that our love is the perfect beat

Write me a love poem

And tell me that I am all you need

And that with you, me and God we are complete

Write me something,

that would bring Maya Angelou to tears

And Shakespeare would be impressed with

Something simply the best

Write me a love note

And I will do the same

And I guarantee you our hearts will be on the same page

SWEET ACQUAINTANCE

Clutched into the distance

trivial games we tend to,

Linking thoughts as if hands

A looping of word play.

Into the abyss away,

charmed presence I reach higher

Forlorn in your charm.

Laying clasped in your arms.

ABOUT THE AUTHOR

Darius Strong is a Black Queer writer and Domestic Violence therapist from Chicago, Illinois. He received his Bachelor's and Master's in both Psychology and Clinical Mental Health Counseling from Northern Illinois University. He has been published in anthologies such as "Soft No.5", "Soft No.6", and "Contemporary Voices". His work explores mental health, Queerness, body positivity, and the many ways these identities converge. Mr. Strong's works shine a light on the resistance to change and growth while acknowledging how rigidness can be seductive but also destructive. As an artist, he recognizes that there is power through lived experiences that challenges you, that challenge your resiliency, and challenges your ability to stay soft.

ABOUT THE AUTHOR

Lola Writes is a Chicago native poet, songwriter, and co-author of her debut book A Letter to You. She has found that true inspiration can be found during the moments of challenge or bliss. She feels that those moments are where you find the greatest stories to be told. Her hope is that her stories are not only relatable, but also says something that can be a life changing moment in someone's life. You can read more of her poetry on her Instagram at @lolawrites10 & you can watch her videos on YouTube at Lola Writes.

ENDNOTES

DEAR READERS,

Thank You...
Thank you for taking the time to read our poems.
Thank you for being our motivation.
Thank you for trusting us.